OCEANSIDE PUBLIC LIBRARY
330 North Hill Street
Oceanside, CA 92054

D0745482

OCEANSIDE PUBLIC LIBRARY

3 1232 00361 9162

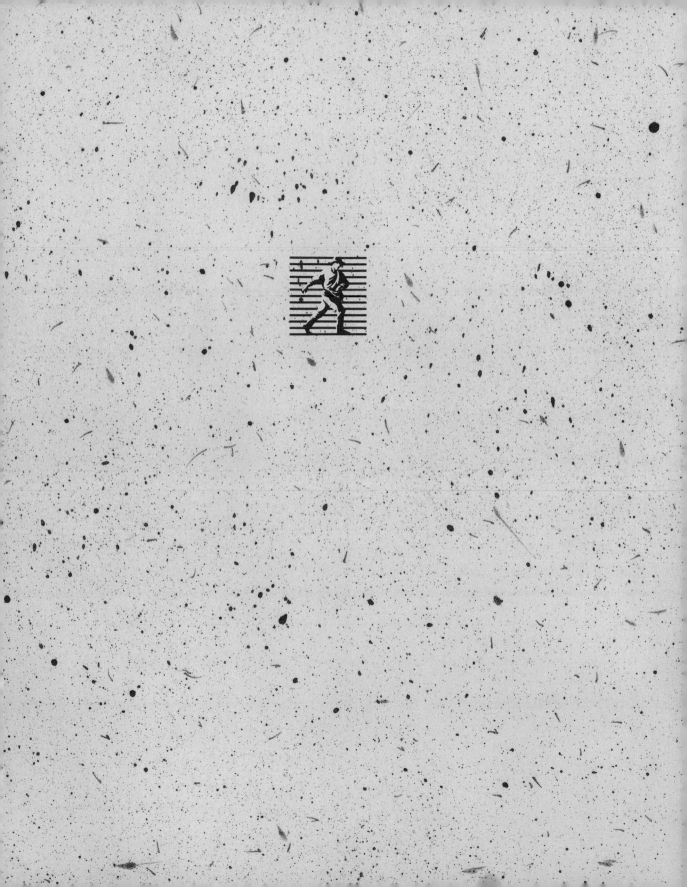

641.59296
PIN

Family of the Spirit Cookbook

Recipes and Remembrances from African-American Kitchens

JOHN PINDERHUGHES

Photographs by John Pinderhughes

SIMON AND SCHUSTER

New York   London   Toronto   Sydney   Tokyo   Singapore

OCEANSIDE PUBLIC LIBRARY
330 North Hill Street
Oceanside, CA 92054

Simon and Schuster
Simon & Schuster Building
Rockefeller Center
1230 Avenue of the Americas
New York, New York 10020

Copyright © 1990 by John Pinderhughes

All rights reserved
including the right of reproduction
in whole or in part in any form.

SIMON AND SCHUSTER *and colophon are registered trademarks*
of Simon & Schuster Inc.

Designed by Karolina Harris
Manufactured in the United States of America

3   5   7   9   10   8   6   4   2

Library of Congress Cataloging in Publication Data
Pinderhughes, John.
Family of the spirit cookbook: recipes and remembrances from African-American kitchens/John
Pinderhughes; photographs by John Pinderhughes.
p.   cm.
Includes index.
1. Cookery, Afro-American.   2. Afro-American cooks—United States.   I. Title.
TX715.P6567   1990

641.59'296073—dc20   90-37577

CIP
ISBN 0-671-67510-9

FEB 2 6 1991

This book is dedicated

to my daughters, Sienna and Ghenet,

who brought a new love and understanding into my life,

and to the memory of my father, John.

Thanks, Dad, for everything.

ACKNOWLEDGMENTS

This book has been simmering for quite some time now. It didn't just happen. It seems as if I've always been in one kitchen or another: sniffing, tasting, watching, asking, and listening. I've learned my food from a lot of wonderful people, people who loved me and shared with me. There have also been an awful lot of people who've helped along the way to make this book idea become a reality. So I'd like to thank:

Gum Gum, Gram T, Aunt C, Frenchy, Damu, Verta, Leah, B.G., Chickie, and Aunt Margie for sharing their love and kitchen with me, for becoming a part of me and allowing me to become a part of them;

My wife, Victoria, who put up with all my mess and still loved and encouraged me;

My daughters, Sienna and Ghenet, who smiled, laughed, made me happy, and ate almost all the food I made for them, though they sometimes needed some prodding;

Mom and Dad, my brothers and their wives, my grandparents, uncles, aunts, cousins, nieces, and nephews, all of my family for the loving atmosphere in which I grew up and continue to live. Thanks for the good times we've had in the kitchen.

Thanks to Carol Darden Lloyd for believing in me and always lending an ear when I needed it;

Malaika Adero, my editor, for her sincere encouragement, for knowing when to prod me and when not to, and for doing it gently.

Elise Goodman, my agent, for not trying to change my book and for lending her ear when I needed it;

Marie Brown for the faith she had in me when I wasn't sure just how to begin and for her direction;

Curtia James for her love of my project and her constant words of encouragement;

Mea Attaway for her constant smile and for loving all my people, as well as for her typing and spelling—because *I can't;*

Cheryl, my sister-in-law, for knowing I could do it and for always loving whatever I cooked;

Friends: Skeeter-Pie, Tank, Ax, Janice, Brent, Joy, Joanne, Kenny, Brickster, Amy, Harry, Sharon B., Jay, Sharon, Herb, Argerie, Al, Bebe, Aaron, Gerri, Adger, Brenda, Nathan, Dr. J, Maryann, Warren, Marie, Donn, Syl, Barbara D., Danny, Lynn, Vince, Laura H., Charlott, Pam, Patricia, Thelma, Carlton, Howard J., Alfreida, Farfel, Evette, Billy, Bob, Carol, Bernard, Lynn, Oz, Brenda, David, Mike, Quincy, Margaret, Charles, Erlene, Christine, and many others, for their love and companionship in the kitchen.

CONTENTS

Bunky   JOHN LLOYD PINDERHUGHES, JR.   13
Gum Gum   GLADYS WASHINGTON
                  PINDERHUGHES   47
Gram T   JULIA ELLEN RUFFIN THOMPSON   77
Aunt C   CAROLYN MILDRED HARDY CASSIO   103
Frenchy   OLIVER WENDELL LESESNE   131
Damu   ERUNDINA PADRON JACOBSON   153
Verta   VERTA MAE SMART-GROSVENOR   177
Leah   LEAH LUCY LANGE CHASE   203
B.G.   BRENDA MARIE GOODWIN   237
Chickie   ENRIQUE ANTONIO RIGGS   265
Aunt Margie MARGARET McCALL THOMAS WARD   289

Index   312

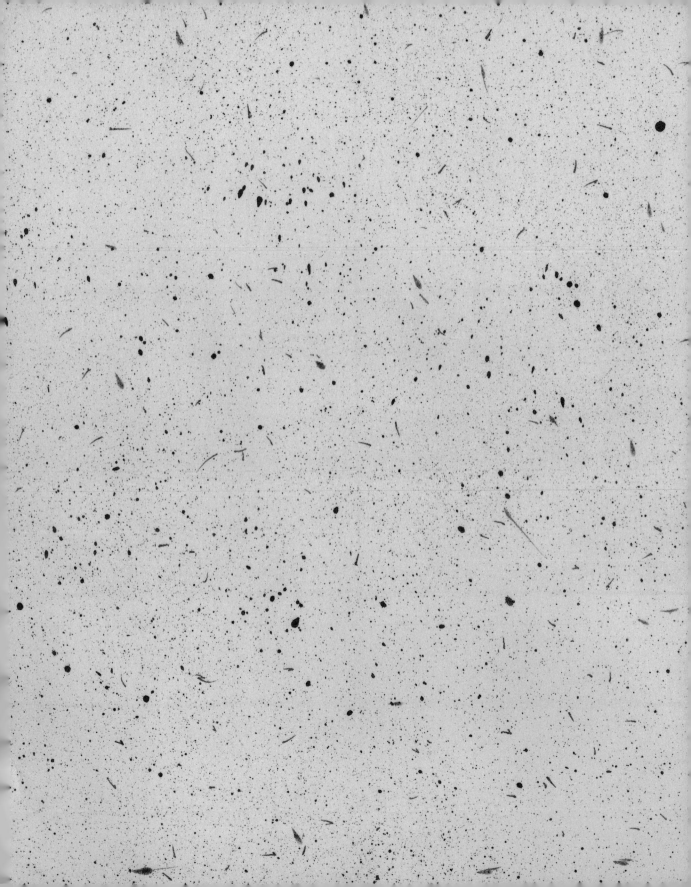

Bunky

JOHN LLOYD PINDERHUGHES, JR.

January 28, 1946   Washington, D.C.

I love to cook. It's like therapy for me, getting in the kitchen, not thinking or worrying about anything else, just cooking. It's great.

I started learning to cook when I was fairly young. My mother only had sons, so when she wanted some time off, we were expected to cook. She made sure both my brothers and I knew how to put something on the table for ourselves. We're not gourmet cooks, mind you, but we can put something on the table.

My true love for cooking began with my grandmother. I really adored her, and when I would be sent to stay with her in the summers, I'd always be right beside her in the kitchen, trying to help. And I did help—just a little. I used to enjoy just anything she would let me do, any little job at all, such as peeling potatoes, trying to shuck oysters, picking tomatoes, or just sitting with her. I grew up liking the kitchen.

Bunky

Sweet Potato-Stuffed Apples
Breakfast Potatoes
Breakfast Rice
Pan Sautéed Soft-Shell Crabs
Pork Chops with Onion and Garlic Gravy
Collard Greens with Tomatoes, Onion, and Garlic
Beet Greens with Pot Liquor
Simple Roast Chicken
Smothered Cabbage
Swiss Chard
Fish Chowder
Fish Stock
Steamed Fish with Shrimp Gravy
Grilled Stuffed Bluefish
Striped Bass Sautéed in Garlic Butter
M. V. Swordfish 1
M. V. Swordfish 2
Spring Scallops
Papaya Flambé
Pan-Fried Porgies for Donn
Mom D's Salad Dressing
Bluefish Cakes
Swiss Chard and Parmesan Omelet
Bunky's Paella
Fran Farmer's Caribbean Pork Roast
Vince Frye's Stuffed Quahogs

Sweet Potato-Stuffed Apples

    4   medium sweet potatoes
    6   tablespoons butter or to taste
    4   tablespoons brown sugar or to taste
    ½   teaspoon salt
    ½   teaspoon freshly ground pepper
    4   Red Delicious apples
    1   lemon
    16 whole cloves
        cinnamon
    2   marshmallows, cut in half

Place the potatoes, unpeeled, in a pot and cover with water. Bring to a boil, lower heat, and cook until they pierce easily with a fork. Drain the potatoes and peel them as soon as they are cool enough to handle. Mash the potatoes in a bowl and add the butter, sugar, salt, and pepper. Mix well and set aside. Meanwhile, scoop out the center of the apples, leaving at least ¼ inch of thickness. Try not to puncture the apple skins. Squeeze lemon juice into and around the insides of the apples. Stick 4 cloves into each apple. Fill the apples with the potato mixture and sprinkle the top with cinnamon. Bake in a pre-heated oven at 325° for 15 minutes. Top with a marshmallow half, return to the oven, and bake until the topping is brown.

Serves 4

Variations: Maple syrup may be used instead of marshmallows. Crushed pineapple may be added to the potato mixture.

Gum Gum was my grandmother, my father's mother. Gum Gum has always been my name for her. She was a lovely, lovely woman. She was warm and loving of her family and all those around her. I spent a lot of time with her growing up. There was no question about it, she was always my favorite grandmother and I was her favorite too. Everyone just knew and accepted that we had a special relationship, even my other grandmother. She'll always have that special place in my heart.

Breakfast was something special in the country. My grandparents, my father's folks, had an old farm in Maryland in a place called Shadyside. I have such fond memories of the whole family gathered there—my family, my uncle and his brood. Most everyone got up real early. My grandfather would be working in the garden or cutting the lawn. Everyone had chores to do, and by nine o'clock the kitchen would be in full swing. Grandpa would make his famous biscuits, someone would fry the ham and bacon, someone else would scramble the eggs. We'd always have fresh sliced tomatoes and cucumbers, and Grandma would always make chipped beef. I can see her now browning the flour so her chipped beef was all brown and nutty flavored and really good. If I was lucky we'd have fried fish and soft-shell crabs as well. The whole family would gather around the dining room table—not a place left empty—and the next hour would be spent laughing, talking, and being together around a wonderful meal.

Breakfast Potatoes

6 large potatoes
½ cup chicken stock
2 tablespoons vegetable oil
2 tablespoons butter
2 cloves garlic, minced
1 medium onion, coarsely chopped
1 small green pepper, minced
1 teaspoon minced parsley
salt, to taste
freshly ground pepper, to taste

Wash and peel the potatoes. Cut the potatoes into ½-inch cubes, placing them in water to keep them from discoloring. Heat the chicken stock in a cast-iron skillet. Drain the potatoes and add to the skillet. Lower the flame and cover, Cook for 15 minutes, turning occasionally. Uncover and add the oil, butter, garlic, onion, green pepper, parsley, salt, and pepper. Turn mixture well. Using a spatula, pat the potatoes down and then turn up the flame a little. Brown the potatoes well on one side. Turn half the pan at a time and brown the other side until good and crusty. Cut into pieces to serve.

Serves 4

Breakfast Rice

4 tablespoons bacon drippings
4 scallions, sliced
2 cups leftover rice
3 eggs, lightly beaten
salt, to taste
freshly ground pepper, to taste

Heat the bacon drippings in a heavy cast-iron skillet. Add the scallions and sauté for several minutes. Add the rice, stirring with a fork to break up the grains. Sauté for 5 minutes, until the rice is hot and starts to take on color. Add the beaten eggs, stirring constantly until the eggs set. Add salt and pepper.

Serves 4

I started fishing when I was around seven or eight—at first with my grandfather, then later they let me go by myself. Everyone knew each other in that community, and someone would always have an eye out for all us kids, plus by the time I was eight years old I was a pretty good swimmer. I would get up with the sun and load my little wagon with my fishing and crabbing stuff and head off for the beach. And I'd fish and crab to my heart's delight. In season I'd roll up my pants and go up into the mud flats, looking for soft-shells which, of course, are regular crabs that have shed the hard shells in order to grow. I was pretty good at finding them and was really quite the little fisherman.

Seems like we always had soft-shell crabs in the morning, sautéed in just a little butter, just as fresh as you can possibly get them. Now that's something special.

Pan Sautéed Soft-Shell Crabs

    8 soft-shell crabs (live, or frozen and thawed)
       salt, to taste
       freshly ground pepper, to taste
    1 teaspoon paprika
    4 tablespoons butter
    1 teaspoon vegetable oil

Clean the crabs by cutting off the face and removing the dead men's fingers, the gills. Rinse the crabs and drain them. Sprinkle the crabs on both sides with salt, pepper, and paprika. Heat the butter and oil in a large cast-iron skillet. When the oil is hot but before the butter burns, add the crabs. Sauté for 3–4 minutes on each side, until they are golden brown. Serve immediately.

Serves 4

Note: Serve with bacon and scrambled eggs for breakfast.

We used to eat tomatoes with almost every meal, especially in the summer when they were at peak season. There's nothing like a tomato fresh off the vine—rubbed with a knife, then peeled—sprinkled with a little salt, pepper, and sugar. Just nothing like it. Except maybe fried green tomatoes with breakfast. Now that's pretty good too.

Sometimes there'd be so many people in the kitchen, I don't see how anything ever got done. We'd all get around the table, and there'd be laughing and talking . . . and more than a little eating too.

Pork Chops with Onion and Garlic Gravy

1	lemon
8	pork chops (½ inch thick)
	salt, to taste
	freshly ground pepper, to taste
1	teaspoon garlic powder
1	cup vegetable oil
1	cup flour
½	teaspoon thyme
½	teaspoon sage
4	tablespoons butter
1	medium onion, chopped
1½	cups water
3	cloves garlic, minced
1	tablespoon minced parsley

Squeeze a little lemon juice over the chops. Sprinkle with salt, pepper, and garlic powder. Set aside for 30 minutes, allowing the meat to come to room temperature. Heat the oil in a large cast-iron skillet. Season the flour with salt, pepper, thyme, and sage. Dredge the chops in the flour and fry slowly 5 minutes per side or until golden brown and done. Set aside. Pour off some of the fat. Add the butter and turn up the flame slightly. Add the onion and sauté for 5 minutes. Add 2 tablespoons of the seasoned flour, stirring constantly to blend well. Add the water and simmer to thicken. Check for salt and pepper. When the gravy is done, add the garlic and parsley. Allow to sit for several minutes, then serve over the chops.

Serves 4

Greens were always popular with my family. My grandfather from Providence, Rhode Island, was a connoisseur of greens. He would eat them all, wild and culti- vated. My grandmother told me how once when they were guests at someone's

house, he saw a field of beautiful dandelion greens, excused himself, and immediately set to picking. My grandmother was really embarrassed but did eat some of the resulting greens.

Collard Greens with Tomatoes, Onion, and Garlic

2 bunches collard greens
¼ pound slab bacon
8 cups water
2 tablespoons vegetable oil
1 large onion, chopped
3 cloves garlic, minced
1 16-ounce can whole tomatoes, drained and coarsely chopped
½ teaspoon red pepper flakes
    salt, to taste
    freshly ground pepper, to taste

Pick the greens, discarding all dead and yellow leaves. Remove the thick stalks. Roll the leaves and slice them. Place them in a sink and cover with water. Wash well to remove all sand and grit. Meanwhile, start the bacon frying in a large pot. Fry for about 5 minutes. Add the water and turn up the flame. Bring to a boil, then lower the flame. Simmer for about 1½ hours, until the liquid has been reduced to about 3 cups. Drain the greens and spin dry. Add the greens to the pot, cover, and simmer for 15 minutes. Remove the cover and simmer for 30 minutes. Meanwhile, heat the oil in a cast-iron skillet. Add the onion and garlic. Sauté for 10 minutes or until the onion wilts. Add the tomatoes, red pepper flakes, salt, and pepper. Mix and simmer for 10–15 minutes. When the greens are almost done and most of the liquid has been absorbed or evaporated, add the tomato mixture. Mix well and simmer, uncovered, for 15 minutes, until the greens are tender and most of the liquid has evaporated.

Serves 6–8

Beet Greens with Pot Liquor

    6 bunches beet greens (tops from 6 bunches of baby beets)
    1 cup water
    4 tablespoons butter
    1 teaspoon minced onion
       salt, to taste
       freshly ground pepper, to taste

Wash the greens well to remove all sand. Place the greens in a medium saucepan and add the water. Cover, bring to a boil, and simmer for 5 minutes. Add the butter, onion, salt, and pepper. Cover again and simmer 5 minutes more. Drain and coarsely chop the greens. Serve the greens as a side dish and the pot liquor (cooking liquid) as a starter, like soup.

Serves 4

Both my grandmothers cooked every day. My mother's mother grew up in Virginia and cooked country style. That's where I got my first taste of chitlins—that ethnic connection, you know. She didn't cook them often, but every once in a while my grandfather would want some, and she would cook them for him. That's where I picked up a taste for chitlins. My mother never acquired a taste for them, but her son definitely did.

Note: For a recipe for chitlins, see page 95.

Simple Roast Chicken

2 small chickens, cut in half
1 lemon
    salt, to taste
    freshly ground pepper, to taste
1 teaspoon thyme
½ teaspoon sage
1 teaspoon rosemary
2 stalks celery, coarsely chopped
½ cup white wine
1 tablespoon minced onion
1 teaspoon minced garlic
6 tablespoons butter

Wash the chicken and pat dry. Squeeze the lemon over the chicken and rub it in slightly. Sprinkle the chicken all over with the salt, pepper, thyme, sage, and rosemary inside and out. Scatter the celery in a greased baking pan and pour in the wine. Place the chicken over the celery and scatter the onion and garlic over the chicken. Cut the butter into patties and place them over the chicken. Place in a preheated oven at 325° and bake for 40–60 minutes, depending on size, or until the juices run clear and the chicken is done. Baste several times during roasting.

Serves 4

Sometime right around Thanksgiving, Grandmother T would get this huge package from Virginia just full of wonderful stuff—such as hams, head cheese, and liver pudding—that I would go crazy over. There was always enough for it to last for weeks and weeks. It would be divided up among the family, so everybody had a share. It was always a magical time.

Smothered Cabbage

1   medium head green cabbage
3   carrots, cut diagonally into ¼-inch slices
3   tablespoons bacon drippings, or as needed
1   medium onion, cut into eighths and separated
1   teaspoon sugar
1   teaspoon vinegar
    salt, to taste
    freshly ground black pepper, to taste

Cut the cabbage into quarters and remove the core. Cut each quarter in half and then slice into ¾-inch slices. Wash and spin or pat dry. Meanwhile, place the carrots in a small saucepan with a little water and gently simmer for 10 minutes. In a heavy cast-iron skillet heat the bacon drippings and add the cabbage. Cover and sauté for 10 minutes, stirring every few minutes. When the cabbage begins to wilt, add the carrots and onion. Sauté another 10 minutes or until tender but still slightly crunchy. Add the sugar, vinegar, salt, and pepper. Mix well. Allow the cabbage to sit for several minutes before serving.

Serves 6

Swiss Chard

2 bunches fresh Swiss chard
8 tablespoons (1 stick) butter
1 clove garlic, minced
1 small onion, minced
   salt, to taste
   freshly ground pepper, to taste

Clean the chard, removing the heavy stalks from the greens. Chop some of the stalks and discard the rest. Wash the greens and spin dry. Heat the butter in a large cast-iron skillet. Add the garlic and onion. Sauté gently until the onion wilts. Add the greens and chopped stalks. Cover the skillet and simmer for 10–15 minutes, until tender. Drain the greens and coarsely chop. Season with salt, pepper, and more butter.

Serves 4

Grandma T baked cakes, that was her thing. She baked all kinds of cakes, pies, and cookies. There was always something sweet in her house. My cousin Tommy and I would always drop by Grandma's, knowing there was always a treat for us.

Fishing is a passion with me. I try to go as often as I can, and that usually turns out to be not enough.

Fish Chowder

¼ pound bacon, cut into ¼-inch dice
8 tablespoons (1 stick) butter
1 cup chopped onion
1 cup chopped celery
1 cup chopped carrots
3 cloves garlic, minced
4 cups fresh fish stock (see page 28)
2 tablespoons flour
4 cups potatoes, cut into ½-inch cubes
2 cups fish (1 fish, 3–4 pounds), cut into ¾-inch pieces (sea trout, striped bass, or flounder)
2 cups heavy cream
   salt, to taste
   freshly ground white pepper, to taste
1 cup sherry or Madeira wine

In a large heavy pot sauté the bacon until almost crisp. Add half the butter, the onion, celery, carrots, and garlic. Sauté about 10 minutes, until the onion wilts. Add the fish stock and bring to a gentle boil. Blend the rest of the butter with the flour and add a little at a time. Add the potatoes and simmer for 10 minutes. Add the fish, stir, and simmer for 5 minutes. Turn off the heat and add the heavy cream. Add salt and pepper. Just before serving add the wine and stir to mix.

Serves 6–8

Fish Stock

    3 pounds fish bones, heads (gills removed), etc.
    1 medium onion, quartered
    1 stalk celery with leaves, coarsely chopped
    4 cloves garlic, smashed
    2 carrots, peeled and coarsely chopped
    ½ cup loosely packed parsley
    3 bay leaves
    1 teaspoon thyme
    1 teaspoon freshly ground black pepper
    ½ teaspoon salt
    3 tablespoons olive oil
    1 cup white wine
    3 quarts water

Place all ingredients in a large stock pot. Bring to a rolling boil. Lower the heat and cook for 15–30 minutes or until reduced to about 8 cups. Strain through cheesecloth and reserve the liquid.

Makes about 8 cups

Steamed Fish with Shrimp Gravy

    1 2–4-pound whole red snapper, gutted and split with the head on
    1 lime
      salt
      freshly ground pepper
    8 cloves garlic, minced
    2 tablespoons white wine vinegar
    1 hot pepper, minced
    2 medium onions, thinly sliced
    1 small green pepper, thinly sliced
    1 pound shrimp
    1 fish head

3   cups water
1   stalk celery
2   tablespoons vegetable oil
1   cup flour
1   bay leaf
½ teaspoon thyme

Wash the fish with the juice of the lime. Rinse, drain, and pat dry. Cut 3 to 4 diagonal gashes in each side of the fish. Cut forward toward the head. Make a mixture of 1 teaspoon of salt, 1 teaspoon of pepper, 2 cloves of garlic, minced, 2 tablespoons of vinegar, and a little of the minced hot pepper. Grind into a paste. Rub the gashes and the inside surfaces with the paste. Place the fish in a flat glass baking dish and cover with the onions (reserving a few), remaining garlic, green pepper, and hot pepper. Marinate for 1 hour. Meanwhile, shell the shrimp, reserving the shells. Coarsely chop the shrimp and set aside. Place the shells and the fish head in a large saucepan with the 3 cups of water and add a little onion and celery. Simmer for 15 minutes. Heat the oil in a large heavy cast-iron skillet. Shake the marinade off the fish and dredge in flour. Fry quickly, 3–4 minutes on each side, until golden brown but not done. Lower the flame and add the marinade vegetables. Pour over 2 cups of the fish stock. Add the bay leaf, thyme, salt, and pepper. Cover and simmer gently for 15–20 minutes. Remove the fish with a slotted spoon and remove the vegetables. Set aside and keep warm. Add 2 tablespoons of flour and stir. Cook slowly, scraping the bottom of the skillet, until the gravy starts to thicken. Strain the gravy and return to the now clean skillet. Add the shrimp and cook until the shrimp turn pink and the gravy is thick. Serve the shrimp gravy over the fish.

Serves 4–6

Fishing trips always seem to be either a bust or an orgy.

I usually go to Martha's Vineyard in late May or early June, just in time for the first runs of bluefish. I just fish and fish some more. My Aunt C and I have a ritual. The first catch is always hers. After I fillet the fish and fill her freezer, I dig up the garden and scatter all the carcasses, bones, and innards. About a week later she plants her tomatoes over the fish. Talk about great tomatoes—tomatoes like you wouldn't believe.

Grilled Stuffed Bluefish

    1 5–7-pound bluefish, split with the backbone removed but with the head left on
    1 teaspoon garlic powder
       salt, to taste
       freshly ground pepper, to taste
    1 lemon
    8 tablespoons (1 stick) butter
    1 cup chopped onion
    ¾ cup chopped celery
    ½ cup chopped green pepper
    3 cloves garlic, minced
    1 pound shrimp, shelled and coarsely chopped
    1 cup white wine
    1 teaspoon thyme
    1 teaspoon basil
    1 teaspoon oregano
    1 cup Italian bread crumbs
    2 cups stuffing mix
    4 slices bacon
    2 tablespoons vegetable oil

Clean and wash the fish. Pat dry. Lay the fish open, skin side down. Sprinkle with garlic powder, salt, and pepper. Squeeze half of the lemon over the fish and set it aside. Melt the butter in a large cast-iron skillet and add the onion, celery, green pepper, and garlic. Sauté about 5 minutes. Add the shrimp, wine, and ½ teaspoon each of the thyme, basil, and oregano, and salt and pepper. Sauté until the shrimp are just pink. Add the bread crumbs and stuffing mix. Mix well. Place 2 slices of bacon in the fish and fold in the shrimp stuffing mixture. Place the other 2 slices of bacon on top of the stuffing mixture and close the fish. Score the fish several times on each side and rub each slit with a mixture of the remaining thyme, basil, and oregano, and salt and pepper. Brush the fish with oil to keep it from sticking. Enclose the fish in a fish basket or griller and place on a grill over white-hot coals and water-soaked mesquite. Squeeze the other half of the lemon over the fish and grill for 10–15 minutes per side, depending on the size of the fish. Test often for doneness. Do not overcook. The fish should have crisp skin and moist, tender flesh.

Serves 6–8

I love bluefish—actually, all fish—but I think my favorite fish is striped bass. The taste is so sweet and delicate. You really have to work to catch 'em, especially if you're fishing off the beach.

Striped Bass Sautéed in Garlic Butter

4 ½-pound fillets of striped bass (1–1½ inch thick)
   salt, to taste
   freshly ground pepper, to taste
4 tablespoons butter
1 teaspoon vegetable oil
3 cloves garlic, smashed

Rinse the fillets and pat dry on paper towels. Sprinkle the fish with salt and a little pepper. Heat the butter and oil in a cast-iron skillet. Add the smashed garlic and sauté until the garlic is golden brown. Remove the garlic and discard. Turn up the flame. When the butter-oil mixture is very hot but just before it burns, add the fish fillets, skin side down. Sauté over a medium-high flame for 5 minutes, until the skin is crisp and brown. Turn the fish and cook 5–7 minutes more, depending on thickness. Do not overcook the fish.

Serves 4

Some fish such as bluefish will stand up to spicing because it has such a strong flavor. Most fish need a more gentle hand when it comes to spices. Swordfish, for example, doesn't need much, nor does weakfish, which has a sweet, delicate flavor. I like to taste the fish, not the spices or the sauce. You don't want to overwhelm the flavor of the fish.

I love swordfish, and years ago while my friends Brent, Joy, and Joanne were visiting me on the Vineyard, I made this dish. Well, Brent wasn't sure he wanted to eat anything called swordfish, so I had to make it really special. I marinated it in a little mayonnaise and mustard, then grilled it outside. After he tasted that fish, he wanted more. We told him that we hadn't saved much for him, seeing as how he had turned up his nose at it. Well, he was fit to be tied, but eventually we gave in and gave him some more.

M. V. Swordfish 1

    4 ½-pound swordfish steaks (¾ inch thick)
       salt, to taste
       freshly ground pepper, to taste
    2 teaspoons dry mustard
    1 tablespoon olive oil
    4 tablespoons mayonnaise
    1 small onion, thinly sliced

Wash the swordfish steaks and pat dry. Using a fork, punch holes in the steaks. Sprinkle with salt and pepper. In a large bowl mix the mustard, olive oil, mayonnaise, and onion. Add the fish and turn to coat. Let stand at room temperature for several hours. Wrap each steak in foil with some of the mayonnaise-mustard-onion mixture. Punch a few holes in the foil packets and place on a grill over white-hot charcoal. Grill for 5 minutes per side, then remove the steaks from the foil and grill several minutes more, until the juices run clear but the center is still slightly pink. Do not overcook.

Serves 4

Note: M. V., Martha's Vineyard.

M. V. Swordfish 2

½ cup olive oil
½ cup soy sauce
  juice of ½ lemon
  grated rind of ½ lemon
2 teaspoons Dijon mustard
2 cloves garlic, minced
⅛ teaspoon red pepper flakes
4 ½-pound swordfish steaks (¾ inch thick)
  salt, to taste
  freshly ground pepper, to taste

Mix together the oil, soy sauce, lemon juice, grated rind, mustard, garlic, and red pepper flakes. Using a fork, punch holes in the steaks. Place the steaks in a glass baking pan and pour the marinade over; turn to coat. Allow the fish to marinate for several hours at room temperature. Grill over white-hot charcoal about 5 minutes per side, until the juices run clear but the center is still slightly pink. Do not overcook. Sprinkle with salt and pepper.

Serves 4

Note: M. V., Martha's Vineyard.

Seems like I've done an awful lot of cooking on the Vineyard; Aunt C and I—and Maryhelen too. We'd have such a great time laughing and cooking. I learned a lot of stuff from them.

Spring Scallops

    1   pound spring bay scallops
    6   tablespoons butter
    ½   teaspoon minced garlic
    1   tablespoon sliced scallions
    1   tablespoon flour
    1   cup white wine
    ½   teaspoon tarragon
        salt, to taste
        freshly ground white pepper, to taste

Rinse scallops and drain. Heat the butter in a heavy cast-iron skillet. Add the garlic and scallions. Sauté for 2–3 minutes. Add the scallops. Sauté for 5 minutes, until the scallops are done. Add the flour, stirring to mix well. Add the white wine, tarragon, salt, and pepper. Simmer slowly until the mixture thickens.

Serves 4

I'm not sure when I started keeping notes and recipes, but I made notes on what I'd seen and cooked. I had lists—who gave me which recipe and how they made it. Over the years I slowly started to pull it all together. Then I got serious. I started looking at it as a book, and that's when I began to actively work on it.

Whenever I would encounter something new or unique, I just had to inquire about it. I've talked my way into many a kitchen. I've been fortunate in knowing and becoming close to lots of wonderful people, many of whom shared not only their love and their lives but their cooking.

There were times in the early years when I was struggling to become a photographer that I didn't have two nickels to rub together. So there were lots of times when I really didn't eat too well, not regularly at least. One of the things I promised myself was that when I did start to make a few dollars, I would always eat whatever I wanted. So you see, I can be a little extravagant with food. I do try to eat well. Living well is the best revenge, or so they say.

Papaya Flambé

2 papayas, ripe but firm
4 tablespoons fresh lime juice
4 tablespoons brown sugar
¼ cup dark rum, cognac, or Grand Marnier
    vanilla ice cream

Cut each papaya in half and scoop out the seeds. Squeeze 1 tablespoon of fresh lime juice over and into each papaya half. Sprinkle each half with 1 tablespoon of brown sugar and allow them to stand for 15 minutes. Place the papayas in a baking dish and then in a preheated oven at 325°. Bake for 15 minutes or until the fruit is quite warm. Meanwhile, heat the rum, cognac, or Grand Marnier in a saucepan. Remove the papayas from the oven and pour the liquor over them. Light with a match and serve flaming. When the flame goes out, add a scoop of ice cream.

Serves 4

I'm not a gourmet cook. I don't cook gourmet food. I don't want peaches on my lobster. I'm just a good cook. Give me the lobster with a little butter.

Food has always been a great way to let people know you care, and when you do, that caring just seems to flow both ways.

Pan-Fried Porgies for Donn

4 medium porgies or red snappers
  salt, to taste
  freshly ground pepper, to taste
2 cloves garlic, minced
1 tablespoon minced parsley
1 lemon
2 cups vegetable oil
1 cup flour

Have the fish gutted but not split, with the heads left on. Wash the fish and pat dry. Cut 3 diagonal slits into the flesh on each side, cutting from the tail toward the head and at an angle. Make a mixture of salt and pepper and rub a little into each slit and the body cavity. Make another mixture of the garlic and parsley. Grind with a pestle until it becomes a paste. Rub a little of the paste into each slit and into the body cavity. Squeeze the lemon over the fish and allow them to sit for 30 minutes. Heat the oil in a large cast-iron skillet until very hot. Dredge the fish in flour and fry over a high flame until crisp outside and moist inside, about 4–5 minutes per side.

Serves 4

Mom D's Salad Dressing

     1 cup olive oil
     ⅓ cup white wine vinegar
     1 tablespoon sugar
     4 cloves garlic, smashed
     1 teaspoon paprika or curry powder
     ¼ teaspoon thyme or basil
        dash of cayenne pepper, or to taste

Place all ingredients in a bottle. Shake well to mix. Reshake before serving.

I was taught not to waste anything—not a thing. Scraps could always help make a stock or leftovers could be turned into another meal. Anytime something got down to the bone, my family would boil that bone and come up with a soup or broth. Nothing was wasted, and that's as it should be.

Bluefish Cakes

4 cups flaked leftover bluefish
1 cup chopped onion
½ cup chopped celery
½ cup chopped green pepper
2 cloves garlic, minced
1 tablespoon minced parsley
½ teaspoon salt
½ teaspoon freshly ground pepper
½ teaspoon dry mustard
1 cup Italian bread crumbs
1 egg, beaten
3 tablespoons mayonnaise
½ cup bacon drippings

In a large mixing bowl combine the fish, onion, celery, green pepper, garlic, parsley, salt, pepper, and mustard with half of the bread crumbs, the egg, and mayonnaise. Mix well and form into loose cakes. Coat evenly with the remaining bread crumbs and set aside for about 30 minutes. Heat the bacon drippings in a heavy cast-iron skillet and fry the cakes slowly over a medium flame until golden brown on both sides.

Serves 4

I don't look at men cooking as a role reversal because I've always cooked. All the years I was a bachelor I cooked for myself. It just seemed to happen that most of the women I got involved with couldn't cook, not one lick. I've often wondered why that was.

I think good cooks just develop a sixth sense. Just a sense of what to throw in and how much . . . what goes with what and what mixes well with what. It's something that can be learned but not taught.

Swiss Chard and Parmesan Omelet

3   tablespoons butter
⅛ teaspoon minced garlic
½ cup leftover Swiss chard
1   egg, lightly beaten
    salt, to taste
    freshly ground white pepper, to taste
1   teaspoon grated Parmesan cheese

Heat 1 tablespoon of butter in a small cast-iron skillet. Sauté the garlic for several minutes. Add the Swiss chard and cook gently until hot. Meanwhile, heat the remaining 2 tablespoons of butter in an omelet pan. Pour in the beaten egg and rotate to coat the sides. When the egg begins to set, place the Swiss chard mixture in the center. Sprinkle with salt, pepper, and grated Parmesan. Fold the sides over and turn the omelet. Cook until done but not burned. Sprinkle with a little salt, pepper, and cheese to serve.

Serves 1

It's amazing how things change. Nowadays all you really have to do is throw something into the microwave and, presto, there's dinner. It's hard to find the time now, or maybe we're not used to taking the time to do things. I'm as guilty as the next person. I'll put things off. People of my grandparents' generation would never do that. When something needed doing, they just did it. No fuss. There was always food in the kitchen, cooked several times a day, and when people dropped by, well, you just had to eat. Food was such a part of social life. If you didn't want anything, then they felt hurt.

Food is very social, at least for me. I'll invite people over. I'll say, "Hey, come on over and have a bite." And I really mean it that way. Come on by and I'll throw something in the pot, and we'll sit down, we'll have a glass of wine, we'll laugh, joke, and have a good time. Share our lives.

Bunky's Paella

½ pound smoked bacon
  salt, to taste
  freshly ground pepper, to taste
5 cloves garlic, minced
2 whole chickens, cut into pieces
4 chorizo sausages, sliced
3 onions, coarsely chopped
1 large green pepper, coarsely chopped
4 stalks celery, chopped
1 bottle dry white wine
1 2-pound can whole tomatoes, coarsely chopped
2 teaspoons bijol (Spanish food coloring) or saffron
1 bay leaf
1 whole live lobster
4 frozen lobster tails, thawed
2 pounds large shrimp
2 dozen littleneck clams
2 dozen mussels
2 pounds rice (or less if you prefer)
1 package frozen green peas
1 4-ounce jar pimentos

Dice the bacon and fry in a large heavy casserole. Fry until almost crisp. Salt and pepper the chicken and rub with garlic. Add the chicken and sausage to the pot and fry for 15 minutes or until the chicken is about half done. Add the onions, green pepper, remaining garlic, and celery. Sauté for 15 minutes or until the onions begin to wilt. Add the wine (½ cup for each cup of rice), tomatoes with their liquid, bijol, salt, pepper, and bay leaf. Cover and simmer until the chicken is almost done. Meanwhile, steam the lobster and cut it into pieces. Cut the lobster tails into pieces. Shell the shrimp. Steam the clams in a little wine until they open. Scrub the mussels. When the chicken is done, remove from the pot and set aside but keep warm. Add the rice and bring the pot to a boil. Add the shrimp. Cover and cook until half the liquid is absorbed. Add the clams, with their liquid, the lobster, lobster tails, and mussels. Cover and cook until all the liquid is absorbed and the mussels have opened. Simmer the green peas until done. Fold the rice and seafood onto a large serving platter and add the warm chicken along with any juices that have accumulated. Garnish with the green peas and pimentos.

Serves 12–15

Fran Farmer's Caribbean Pork Roast

- 1 4–5-pound boneless pork roast
- 2 cloves garlic, sliced
- 1 teaspoon ginger
- 1 teaspoon allspice
- 1 teaspoon garlic powder
- 1 teaspoon herb pepper (Spice Island)
- 1 teaspoon coriander
- 1 teaspoon seasoned salt

Punch holes in the roast and insert the slices of garlic. Make a mixture of the remaining ingredients and rub it over and into the roast. Allow the roast to sit for 1 hour, then roast in a preheated oven at 350° for about 1 hour. Make a paste of the following:

- ½ cup light brown sugar
- ¼ cup dark rum
- 2 cloves garlic, minced
- 2 bay leaves, crushed
- ½ teaspoon ginger
- ½ teaspoon allspice
- 1 teaspoon lime juice

Spread the paste onto the roast and continue roasting at 350° until a meat thermometer indicates just done for pork. Drain the pan drippings, degrease, and thicken, adding a little water if necessary. Serve over the sliced meat.

Serves 6–8

Vince Frye's Stuffed Quahogs

12 quahogs
    water
1   pound linguica (Portuguese sausage)
1   medium onion, chopped
1   medium green pepper, chopped
4   tablespoons vegetable oil
2   cloves garlic, minced
1   tablespoon chopped parsley
1   cup Italian bread crumbs
1   egg, lightly beaten
    salt, to taste
    freshly ground black pepper, to taste
    dash of cayenne pepper
1   tablespoon paprika

Scrub the quahogs and steam them in 2 inches of water until they open. Remove the clams from the shells and chop them. Save the shells. Skin the linguica and grind in a meat grinder. Sauté the onion, green pepper, and garlic in the oil until the onion starts to wilt. Remove from the heat. Add the parsley, bread crumbs, egg, salt, pepper, and cayenne pepper. Add the chopped clams and the linguica. Mix well. Lightly oil the shells and stuff with the quahog mixture. Sprinkle paprika over the top of each. Bake in a pre-heated oven at 375° for 25 minutes. Serve hot.

Serves 6

I'm real lucky. I grew up with a lot of love, and food was always a part of that.

Gum Gum

GLADYS WASHINGTON PINDERHUGHES

November 11, 1892   Baltimore, Maryland.

Gum Gum is my paternal grandmother. My first memories of food and family cooking are from her kitchen. My first attempts at helping to cook were nurtured by her. My grandmother was a warm, loving woman in the old-fashioned sense who taught the values of love, caring, family, and hard work. I'm lucky to have had her.

Gum Gum

Gum Gum's Crab Cakes
Seafood Casserole
Oyster Fritters
Scalloped Oysters
Deviled Crab-Stuffed Flounder
Deviled Crabs
Creamed Chipped Beef
Chipped Beef and Eggs
Kidney Stew
Simple Leg of Lamb
Lamb Shanks
Ham Croquettes
Grandpa's Famous Leftover Steak Hash
Fried Tomatoes
Sliced Tomatoes
Green Tomato Pickle
Gee's Watermelon Pickle
Gee's Cole Slaw
Everyday Cucumber Salad
Sweet Potato and Orange Casserole
Leftover Yam Pudding
Corn Patties
Spanish Rice
Charlie's Biscuits
Macaroon Ice Cream

I was born in Baltimore, November 11, 1892, on a little street called Rose Street. It doesn't even exist anymore, it's all built up with state buildings on it.

My earliest recollection of cooking? Well, I guess I was ten years old. I made bread. It was such a joke. My sister Maude—a sleepyhead—was supposed to tell me how to make the bread dough. She did, and I put everything on the table to begin and I said, "How much salt, Maude?" She told me a cup, so I put a cup of salt in the dough. The next morning when my mother came down to bake the bread and rolls, the dough was just as flat as I had left it the night before. I told her I did just what Maude had told me. She liked to had a fit, 'cause we couldn't afford to throw out a whole batch of bread. We had to, though, because it wasn't any good.

We never had pigtails, and we never had—what do you call those things?—chitlins. Now I call that Southern. We had oysters, crabs, and lots of fish—sea trout and those little flat fish. We called them diamonds, but there's another name for them. We had shad, in season. My papa loved that, but in those days I didn't like shad 'cause I couldn't stand all the bones. Nowadays you can buy shad filleted.

Well, Mama did what I guess you'd call general cooking, and Dad, he could cook pretty good too. If he was home in the morning, he would show me how to fix little things, like maybe the bacon. He knew about a little higher grade of cooking than we ordinarily had. Every morning he cooked he'd add some little extra touch.

Gum Gum's Crab Cakes

1   pound lump or backfin crab meat
1   small onion, finely minced
2   tablespoons bread crumbs
1   teaspoon salt
1   teaspoon freshly ground pepper
1   teaspoon dry mustard
1   egg, lightly beaten
4   tablespoons mayonnaise
   flour, for dusting
   bacon fat or vegetable oil

Pick the crab meat, removing all shell and hard pieces but being careful not to break up the crab meat too much. In a bowl mix together the crab meat, minced onion, bread crumbs, salt, pepper, mustard, egg, and mayonnaise. Fold lightly in your hand, making sure not to compress the cake too much. The crab cake should just hold together. Sprinkle with flour and fry slowly in bacon fat or light vegetable oil until golden brown.

Serves 4

Seafood Casserole

1   pound lump or backfin crab meat
½ pound shrimp
½ cup white wine
½ pound bay scallops
8   tablespoons (1 stick) butter
1   large onion, finely chopped
½ large green pepper, finely chopped
½ cup finely chopped celery
2   eggs
1   can cream of mushroom soup
1   teaspoon dry mustard
1   teaspoon freshly ground white pepper
    bread crumbs

Pick the crab meat, removing all shell and hard pieces. Steam the shrimp in a little white wine and chop coarsely. Sauté the scallops in a little butter and add to the crab meat and shrimp. Set the seafood mixture aside. In a saucepan heat half the butter and add the onion, green pepper, and celery. Sauté until they begin to wilt. Add the remaining butter and sauté 10 minutes more. Beat the eggs and add to the saucepan, stirring constantly. Add the cream of mushroom soup, mustard, and pepper, and stir. Place the seafood mixture in a casserole and pour the sauce over it. Sprinkle the top with bread crumbs. Place the casserole in a large deep baking pan to which about 2 inches of hot water have been added. Place the whole thing in a preheated oven and bake at 375° for 1 hour. Allow to cool slightly before serving.

Serves 4–6

My mother made oyster pie, a delicious oyster pie. And she would make scalloped oysters too. But of course I didn't like oysters when I was growing up. But then I learned to like them. Yes, I learned to love them, really. I was grown before I would even taste them. But now . . .

Oyster Fritters

½ pint fresh shucked oysters
1 teaspoon salt
1 cup flour, sifted
1 teaspoon baking powder
1 egg, beaten
1 cup milk
2 tablespoons oil

Drain the oysters and place them in a bowl. Sprinkle with ½ teaspoon of salt and set aside. In another bowl mix the flour, remaining salt, baking powder, egg, and milk into a batter. Add the oysters to the batter. Heat the oil in a frying pan or on a griddle. Spoon out small amounts of the batter as you would for pancakes but with an oyster or two in each. Fry until golden brown.

Serves 4

Scalloped Oysters

    unsalted buttter
1 cup crushed soda crackers or Italian bread crumbs
1 quart oysters
    celery salt, to taste
    freshly ground pepper, to taste
1 can cream of mushroom soup

Rub the butter in a deep baking dish or casserole. Add a layer of crushed crackers or bread crumbs, then a layer of oysters. Sprinkle with celery salt and pepper. Repeat until the casserole is almost full. In a saucepan warm the soup without adding milk or water. When liquefied pour over the mixture in the baking dish. Add a few more crumbs. Bake in a preheated oven at 350° for about 1 hour or until well set.

Serves 4

I think my mother was an excellent cook, but I didn't really appreciate her cooking until I was in high school. My first year in high school I began to take notice. In those days we had a coal stove. It wasn't until much later that we got gas. It seems I've lived through so many eras. You know things were different in the 1890s and early 1900s. Each ten or twenty years seems so different, a different era. When I was little we didn't have planes and such, but now . . .

Deviled Crab-Stuffed Flounder

6 tablespoons butter
2 tablespoons flour
1 teaspoon salt
1 teaspoon dry mustard
½ teaspoon Worcestershire sauce
¼ teaspoon garlic powder
2 teaspoons lemon juice
    freshly ground pepper, to taste
    dash of Tabasco
⅔ cup milk
2 cups picked crab meat
8 flounder fillets
    bread crumbs

In a saucepan melt 3 tablespoons of butter. Blend in the flour, salt, mustard, Worcestershire sauce, garlic powder, 1 teaspoon lemon juice, pepper, and Tabasco. Blend well. Gradually add the milk, stirring constantly until the mixture thickens. Add the crab meat and mix well. Sprinkle the fillets with a little salt and pepper and arrange 4 of them in a greased baking dish. Spread ¼ of the crab mixture over each fillet and top with the remaining 4 fillets. Melt the remaining 3 tablespoons of butter and add the remaining lemon juice. Pour a little over each fillet. Sprinkle with bread crumbs. Bake in a preheated oven at 350° for 20–30 minutes, until the fish just flakes with a fork. Cut the fillets in half to serve.

Serves 8

Grandpa would never eat crabs the way most people would, breaking those hard shells, biting and sucking 'em the way they do. He didn't like 'em that way. He would sit down with a bowl, a napkin, and a knife and fork, and just pick all the meat out into that bowl. And then when he had finished, he would season it with a dash of salt, pepper, and mayonnaise, almost like we did the crab cakes. People used to laugh at him about it, but that's the way he was.

Deviled Crabs

1   pound crab meat
½ cup bread crumbs
1   egg, lightly beaten
¼ cup minced celery
¼ cup minced onion
¼ cup minced green pepper
1   teaspoon dry mustard
1   teaspoon Worcestershire sauce
1   teaspoon freshly ground pepper
1   teaspoon salt
2   tablespoons lemon juice
½ cup mayonnaise
    dash of Tabasco

Pick the crab meat, removing all shell and hard pieces. Mix all the ingredients together well and fold into individual crab shells or bakery molds. Place in a preheated oven at 350° for 15–20 minutes.

Serves 6

Everybody always loved my chipped beef, or said they did. When our friends came down to Shadyside, they always talked about the chipped beef. We used to serve it two ways: with scrambled eggs and creamed.

Well, let's see now, we'd take what would be about a half package [of chipped beef] and put about two tablespoons of oil to heat in a skillet. We'd never use bacon fat in the chipped beef; the beef was already salty, and I don't like too much salt, though one friend of mine tells me that I used to use bacon fat down in the country. But I don't remember that. It could be that the chipped beef we got down there wasn't as salty. And I would break up the chipped beef and put it into the pan to brown. Keep movin' it around so's it wouldn't burn or dry out too much. Then I'd take, for half a package, oh . . . about three eggs. Beat them and stir them into the chipped beef while the pan was hot, and when they were just done, I'd add some pepper.

Creamed Chipped Beef

3 ounces chipped beef (sliced dried beef)
3 tablespoons oil or butter
3 tablespoons flour
1 pint milk

Break the beef into small pieces and set aside. Heat the oil or butter in a skillet. Add the beef and brown; do not let the beef burn. Remove the beef. Add the flour, stirring constantly and cooking until it turns golden brown. (A little extra oil may be needed.) When the flour has turned golden, add the milk and beef. Cook slowly until it thickens. Serve over toast.

Serves 4

Oh, how I remember those big breakfasts we used to have in the country. What with all the kids and grands and friends and family. People still write me and express what delightful times they had there. They said it was such a fun place, a place where you could relax and enjoy yourself. And one of the things people mentioned the most was how they enjoyed the breakfasts.

Chipped Beef and Eggs

    2   tablespoons oil or bacon fat
    1   4-ounce package chipped beef
    6   large eggs
        freshly ground pepper, to taste

Place the oil or bacon fat in a frying pan and heat over low heat. Break up the chipped beef and add it to the pan. Brown slowly, keeping the beef moving so it will not burn. Crack and lightly beat the eggs. When the beef is lightly browned, add the eggs and pepper, mix well, and cook until just firm.

Serves 3–4

Now, if you're talking about breakfast, kidney stew was always a favorite.

Kidney Stew

8   small kidneys (lamb or veal)
2   teaspoons salt
1   medium onion, coarsely chopped
1   stalk celery with leaves, coarsely chopped
6   tablespoons butter
3   tablespoons flour
3   medium potatoes, cut into ½-inch cubes
1   teaspoon celery salt
   freshly ground pepper, to taste

Soak the kidneys for 3–6 hours in water to which 1 teaspoon of salt has been added. Drain the kidneys and add fresh water to cover and another teaspoon of salt. Add the onion and the celery. Bring to a boil, lower the heat, cover, and simmer for 30 minutes. Allow the kidneys to cool. Remove and cut into ½-inch cubes. Set aside. Strain the cooking liquid and set that aside also. In a large saucepan melt the butter and add the flour. Cook, stirring constantly, until the flour turns golden brown. Add the strained liquid and cook slowly until it thickens. At the same time boil the potatoes until almost done. Drain the potatoes and add them to the thickened cooking liquid along with the cubed kidneys. Season with celery salt and pepper. Simmer gently for 10–15 minutes.

Serves 6

Leg of lamb was a favorite of mine. I didn't know for years why my mother always had that little hole made in the leg of lamb. I asked the butcher once and he told me. "Well, your mother had the gland taken out," he said. "It's something a lot of people don't like, and your mother was one of them." Some people claim that the gland makes the meat tough if it stays inside. And so I used to always have that little gland taken out. And I like to put a little salt in the hole just like my mother. No garlic then; I didn't like garlic until I met your grandfather Charlie. After him I started to like it. You always have to cut the skin off the lamb, and the stamp, rub it with a little grease and salt. Years ago we didn't have racks to put the meat on. Later I got a rack, and Mama enjoyed using that rack so much. You see, the meat didn't stick or anything.

Simple Leg of Lamb

    1 5-pound leg of lamb
    2 tablespoons vegetable oil
    1 clove garlic, smashed
    1 lemon
       salt, to taste
       freshly ground pepper, to taste

Have the fell (the membrane on a leg of lamb) and any excess fat cut away. Place the oil in a small bowl and add the garlic. Allow the garlic to sit in the oil for about 1 hour. Meanwhile, rub the meat with the juice of half a lemon. Let the meat sit long enough to come to room temperature. Rub the meat all over with the garlic oil. Sprinkle with salt and pepper. Place the meat on a rack, fat side up, in an uncovered greased baking pan. Place the pan in a preheated oven at 500° and roast for 15 minutes, then lower the heat to 325° and continue roasting for 1 hour. Check the meat at the end of an hour by cutting into it to see if it is done enough for your taste. (Use a meat thermometer if you desire.)

Serves 6

Nowadays you put everything in the refrigerator, but in days past we didn't have electric. We had to get ice every day. Our box held what they called fifty pounds. A big block would last maybe two days. Things are a lot different now.

We were taught never to waste anything. If you had mashed potatoes one night, you had potato cakes the next. If you had a leg of lamb one or two nights, the third day you made stew.

Lamb Shanks

4 meaty lamb shanks
2 cloves garlic, smashed
½ cup flour
2 tablespoons vegetable oil
1 cup chopped onion
2 cups meat stock
2 teaspoons salt
½ teaspoon freshly ground pepper
1 bay leaf
2 cups crushed tomatoes
½ cup chopped carrots
¼ cup chopped celery
¼ cup chopped green pepper
1 large potato, cut into ½-inch cubes

Rub the shanks all over with the garlic and reserve the garlic. Dredge the shanks in flour. Heat the oil in a large heavy casserole and sear the meat. Add the onion and continue cooking until the shanks are browned on all sides. Pour off the fat and add the meat stock, salt, pepper, garlic, and bay leaf. Cover and bake in a preheated oven at 325° for 1 hour or until tender. Add the tomatoes, carrots, celery, green pepper, and potatoes. Cover and cook 30 minutes more or until the meat is almost falling off the bones and the vegetables are done. If the cooking liquid has thickened enough, use it as a gravy with the shanks and vegetables. If not, strain off some of the liquid and thicken it.

Serves 4

Ham Croquettes

2 cups ground leftover ham
1 teaspoon Dijon mustard

1   can cream of celery soup
1   egg
2   tablespoons milk
1   cup bread crumbs
2   cups vegetable oil
½ cup crumbled cheddar cheese

In a bowl combine the ham, mustard, and half the soup. Blend well and chill for 30 minutes or so. Shape into 8 croquettes. Dip each croquette in a mixture of the egg and milk, then coat with the bread crumbs. Heat the oil in a large frying pan and fry the croquettes until they are golden brown. Drain the croquettes on paper towels. Heat the remaining soup in a saucepan and add the cheese. Thin with milk if necessary. Spoon over the croquettes to serve.

Serves 4

Grandpa's Famous Leftover Steak Hash

4   tablespoons bacon fat
3   large potatoes, cut into ½-inch cubes
1   medium onion, chopped
2   cloves garlic, minced
½ cup beef gravy or stock
3   cups cubed leftover steak
    salt, to taste
    freshly ground pepper, to taste
    dash of Tabasco

Heat the bacon fat in a large frying pan. Add the potatoes, onion, and garlic. Cook over a medium flame, turning occasionally, until potatoes are just tender. Add the gravy or stock, leftover steak, salt, pepper, and dash of Tabasco. Turn up the flame slightly and cook until the potatoes have browned and the meat is hot.

Serves 4

Greens—they were one of my husband's specialties. He loved all kinds, even what I would call weeds. Down in Shadyside he'd go out and pick all kinds of things. He'd come back with a mess of dandelions or poke salad and he'd handle them so lovingly, picking through them so carefully, gently washing them. Wild greens always seemed bitter to me, but he'd parboil them first and let them sit in some hot water to take out that bitter taste. I guess it worked 'cause everyone just loved his greens. He liked his greens rich, you know. Seasoned well. No salt pork, mind you —he felt that was tasteless—but a leftover ham bone or slab of bacon was just what the doctor ordered.

Yes, we fried tomatoes, not green ones, mind you, but nice, firm, ripe ones. Laura (my grandmother's cousin) knows how much I like them. Every time I go there, she has fried tomatoes waiting; she just spoils me so!

Fried Tomatoes

    4 large tomatoes, sliced into ½-inch slices
       salt, to taste
       freshly ground pepper, to taste
    ½ cup flour
    4 tablespoons bacon fat
    2 tablespoons sugar
    2 tablespoons butter

Wash tomatoes and slice. Sprinkle with salt and pepper, then dredge in flour, trying not to handle the slices too much. Heat the bacon fat in a frying pan.

When the bacon fat is hot, add the tomatoes and brown on both sides. As the tomato slices are done, remove to a serving platter, sprinkle with sugar, and dot with butter. (If you desire, deglaze the frying pan with 2 tablespoons of water and pour this over the tomatoes.

Serves 6

Sliced Tomatoes

3 large, firm, ripe tomatoes
1 medium sweet onion, thinly sliced
  salt, to taste
  freshly ground white pepper, to taste
  sugar, to taste
  vegetable oil or mayonnaise

Rub the skin of the tomatoes with the dull edge of a knife until the skin wrinkles, then peel it off. Slice the tomatoes ½ inch thick and arrange with the sliced onion. Sprinkle with salt, pepper, and just a little sugar. Serve by themselves or with salad oil or mayonnaise.

Serves 4

I don't know why we peeled the tomatoes. That's the way we did it, that's all.

My mother used to make the most delicious pickle out of green tomatoes. I can smell it now. All day long she would be cooking, wrapping her spices in little bits of cheesecloth. She never liked to have the spices loose in the pickle; she didn't like biting on those bits of spice. All the tomatoes, onions, and spices would be in this huge kettle. All the neighbors wanted some after she cooked a batch, and of course she gave.

Green Tomato Pickle

2 dozen green tomatoes, sliced
3 medium green peppers, sliced
3 medium onions, sliced
4 cloves garlic, smashed
1 cup sugar
2 tablespoons salt
1 quart vinegar
1 ounce pickling spices

Place the tomatoes, green peppers, onions, garlic, sugar, salt, and vinegar in a large pot and mix well. Wrap the pickling spices in cheesecloth to form a bouquet and add to the pot. Bring to a boil, lower the heat, and simmer for 3 hours, stirring every 20 minutes. Use the side of the spoon to break up any large pieces. Turn off the heat and allow to cool somewhat. Remove the bouquet and place the mixture in mason jars. Refrigerate. Serve cold.